Running from the Pack

Pack

2015/16 Savant Poetry Anthology

Edited by Helen R. Davis

Savant Books and Publications
Honolulu, HI, USA
2016

Published in the USA by Savant Books and Publications
2630 Kapiolani Blvd #1601
Honolulu, HI 96826
http://www.savantbooksandpublications.com

Printed in the USA

Edited by Helen R. Davis
Cover Art and Design by Daniel S. Janik

ISBN/EAN: 9780996325554

Table of Contents
(in order of occurrence)

Dylan DiMarchi

Dylan is a 17-year-old high-school student who has a passion for filmmaking and engineering. And writing, of course. Dylan developed his writing under the guidance of his inspiring teacher Joe Tsujimoto, a published author of prose and poetry. This poem was one of many Dylan composed in a single, hand-written book of his most memorable creations.

Running from the Pack
by Dylan DiMarchi

Remember that time
When you had a chance to make a difference?
But you stayed with the pack
Your invisible leash of fear
Holding you back

Or when you saw that one
Alone
Bravely stand for independence
You hung your head in shame
The bindings of your leash
Tight as ever

We, the few
Declare our independence
From those who attack and demean
Those of us who dare to be different
Their chains of conformity wrap around our legs
But we break free from their shackles

I turn into the wind
They drift with the current
I choose the high peak
They choose the valleys

I seek the faster way
The better way
The newer way, to improve
They scoff
"Why change?"

They follow one another
Like a line of ants
Unsure of their path
Bumping along
Content to blindly follow

We, the few
Walk our own route
The road might be lonely
And filled with hills and valleys
But it is the road we choose
Honor our decision
To be different
And separate from the whole

We choose this way
To follow our dreams
Skirting the slow
Monotonous line of ants
On our way to our future
Creating our own route

Call us different
Unusual
Strange
But we call ourselves the leaders
The path makers
The dreamers

Teuta S. Rizaj

Teuta S. Rizaj was a professor and an educator for many years both in the U.S. and overseas. She is the author of *The Rhapsody of the Ant Woman: Poem with Complimentary Drawings & The Sliced Land and Other Stories*. She has also translated and authored nonfiction books, book reviews, articles, and studies. Apart from writing, Rizaj also enjoys drawing and painting, and the company of the seekers of Truth.

The Scarecrows
by Teuta S. Rizaj

I wish I had a field with seven grains
With high-pointed mountains surrounded,
And by a quiet, rippling stream,
I wish I had a house I dream.

Scarecrows there I wish to make
From my grandfathers' old ragged clothes—
Worn and torn in their battlefields;
Drenched and washed with their tears.

Scarecrows at day shall scare away
Attacks of flocks of hungry crows;
At night the scarecrows shall celebrate
Their vigilant labor of the day—

Singing and dancing with mothers and fathers,
Sons and daughters of my grandfathers
Around the high-leap, golden fire-flames.

Life-giving rains shall help the grains
To weave the threads of ample harvest—
Reaped and gathered in late summer
And stored with warmth for cold winter.

Say, hail, hail to heedful scarecrows

Who saw and see on each table
Food to be placed each cool morning—
Thus proving their kind worthy and able.

Uhene

So I live in the beautiful, paradise state of Hawaii, single, no kids, love people, females especially. Dearly love any food with the flavor of the mango fruit. Grandfather Kawika took me to my first theater movie at five years of age, a samurai production. Wow!

Einstein's Formula of Relativity Verses Uhene's Formula of Reality
by Uhene

Uhene's Formula Of Reality:

$$P=Q \text{ to } A \text{ is } B$$

If what comes after P is Q , which is the Question, what comes before B is A, which is the Answer, then what is B?

B is the belief, needed to have a thought that demonstrates the Question and, since with a Question there is an Answer, the Answer is to believe in the Only Son of the Most High God , Jesus!

> By the Pen of the Holy Spirit
> Dedicated to Grandfather Kawika,
> Dad Bobby and My Lord and Savior, Jesus

Marianne Smith

Marianne Smith is a wife to Roger, mother to Shawn and Jacob, and loving aunt to Helen Davis, the editor of this anthology.

First Steps
by Marianne Smith

When love is fresh and new
it's center is brightly shining
It sparkles like champagne
yet as it slowly stretches and grows
it becomes deeper and fuller
as a fine wine, patiently, with age,
its taste is lush, rich and fully fragrant
Tenderly, softly, love's first steps of courtship grow
carefully learning of each one to the other
how much they feel, joy they have never known
delightfully as love rushes in, it
engulfs their minds with awe & wonder
overflowing it has blossomed and grown

The two hearts meld and vows are heard
in a bond of matrimony
their eyes locked into a secret place
that just the two of them share
When times get rough on the journey
that lies before them
they can take the steps to seek solution
and find within their sacred place
no other can tear asunder
a enduring ever lasting peace
their love was meant to find.

Danny Smith

Originally from Chicago, Illinois, Danny Smith is a son, father, friend and poet who currently resides in the Virginia Beach, area. Danny lives with his three children, Katie, Beth and Noah, as well as other family and friends. His favorite poet is Edgar Allan Poe, the biggest influence on writing was his tenth grade teacher Ms. Archibald at Western Branch High School, and his favorite pub, the South Beach Grill.

Placing Emotion in His Words
by Danny Smith

When the words were written
The poet felt each one
Inside of their meaning
Was a hope the quest was done
He knew if he wrote of love
And all the dreams he dreamt
That someday one who felt as he
Would feel his words as meant
He believed that his vision
Was prophetic in its cause
That he could never stop
Or for that matter pause
For life was fleeting
There had been far too many nights
When his arms were empty
Which is darkness in light
And pray yes he prayed
That the words would soon be seen
By the love of his life
That he only knew in his dreams
Awaiting such a love
He sat then to write
Placing emotion in his words
Hoping she will read them tonight…

Manal Hamad

a freelance translator and poet and sometimes i do
art criticism as well

Poppy Tears
by Manal Hamad

Poppy tears
They say…
They contain opium
Those fragile red.
Fluttering petals…
A dark stem
Bearing a red cup…
Sylvia Plath liked
Them.
I looked at the poppies
Not in a field
Of some French impressionist painter
In my Facebook
Page…
You sent me some…
Do I like you?
Do you like me…?
The eternal question
Posed…
In the wrong moment.
I looked at the dancing
Poppy…
Dews collect
Slip

And recollect
As my memories
Of you…
"Stupid"
You called me once…
Why send a stupid
Girl
Poppies…?

Thomas Koron

Thomas Koron was born in Grand Rapids, Michigan on May 19, 1977. He has attended Grand Rapids Community College, Aquinas College, Western Michigan University and the American Conservatory of Music. He remains active in Grand Rapids as a writer, composer and performer.

The Fading Scent of Perfume
by Thomas Koron

In the deepest memories of my mind,
There is a place to where I wish to go.
Remembering a woman fair and kind,
I miss her more than she will ever know.
And yet, I still find myself asking how
It is we could have passed each other by.
Although, I cannot think about that now;
She disappeared without a reason why.
The air is still, and she has gone away;
I sit and wonder where this woman went.
Hoping we meet again another day;
For each moment with her is time well spent.
 Now, my tearful eyes scan this empty room,
 That's filled with the fading scent of perfume.

J. Okajima

I am a writer who writes straight from the heart about things that inspire me. I have been writing for many years as a source of relaxation and dreaming my goals.

The First Time I Saw You from Afar
by J. Okajima

I loved you from the first day we met
Your smile,
Your touch of your eyes,
You holding my gaze,
You captured my heart.
You have been the one I was looking for
The only one I could not speak a word too
Just smile as we passed by every day.
I felt the love for you yet you were too shy to return it!

The Days of Old
by Thomas Koron

When I now look out far over the hills,

Fondly remembering the days of old;

I see snow on the ground, and my mind fills

With the numbness of twenty winters' cold.

I reflect upon the happiest times;

Sitting in the sun with my closest friends,

But as we age, our faces fill with lines;

Like trees turning bare after summer ends.

The harsh wind blows, it leaves our cheeks glow-
ing;

Breaking from an innocence that won't last.

Hairs start to grey and we begin growing

Increasingly frail as time travels past.

    Moments we keep for the rest of our lives,

    Preserving reminiscence that survives.

A. G. Hayes

Multi-award winning author A. G. Hayes studied television writing at UCLA and has published four novels, numerous short fiction works, including "Cover up," "Not a Penny Pincher," "Home," "Payment in Full," "Small Wonder," "Guided Through a Mine Field" and other scripts to CBS TV and other television productions, as well as poetry. He lives in Northern California, and spends his time writing and traveling to nearly every part of the world. He uses personal experiences gained during service with British intelligence in Eastern Europe and the Middle East to enrich the characters of his works. Savant publications include WHO'S KILLING ALL THE LAWYERS? (2011), THE JUDAS LIST (2012), IMMINENT DANGER (2013) and THE CHEMICAL FACTOR (2015).

Secret Places
by A. G. Hayes

Secret places only I know, inside my mind.
Friendly places perhaps I should share with others.
A place I used to observe the wind and gulls,
Their wings outstretched,
Eyeing me as I sprawled on the cliff top,
Smelling the sea.
Below, the town, my house with grey slate roof,
Warm within,
With the aroma of fresh baked bread.
In time I would return.
Inside my mind, I watched,
Cold to the bone,
As the winter sun sank grey into a grey north sea.
Then stiffly I stood and shouted loudly to no one,
Yelling into the stiff wind.
Before ambling down the crumbling earthen path
home.
Inside my mind, I told myself I was a soldier.
I would return from war,
And to my secret places on the cliff,
Observing the wind and the sea,
Not knowing,
I would soon be a soldier going to war.
Places I should share with others.
Friendly places perhaps, I should share with others.
But are there any such places left,
Or persons who would understand?

Kelsea Kennedy

Kelsea Kennedy is a high school student and aspiring author.

Ephemeral Kiss
by Kelsey Kennedy

If I could die in endless bliss,

Then it would be, from the taste

Of your ephemeral kiss.

One day I happened to meet you,

Now I'll never ever forget,

How you've never left me blue.

When I decided to tell you my story,

You sat down and cried,

Listening when I spoke of the mourning glory.

Here for one single day,

Dead in the next,

Always in the worst way.

To my surprise you sat there,

Then you spoke to me,

"Why is your life so unfair?"

I really don't know,

There is never anything left,

Therefore there is nothing to show.

Someone abused cried for me,

And I for you,

Though I wish you could see.

Two messed up people,

Two wounded souls

Two here to keep this from evil.
In the light, tomorrow comes,
All through the night,
I can only hum.
So for me, eternal bliss,
Lies in the sweet taste,
Of your ephemeral kiss.

C. P. Little

I am rural Irish man living in the heart of a Mediterranean metropolis.

An Elegy for Rising Fears for the Stability of Northern Ireland
by C. P. Little

Fretful, green-eyed-pulse fury from a recent past,
Receding backwards out of consciousness, resolute-
ly.

Reseeding, sprouting, then gyring, up up up up up
beyond
The petite grievance that stewed in the pressure
cooker for six
Decades, where
Bomb
   Nail
    Siren
     Collusion
      Tout-stained
tastelessness left my blood pox-marked with
IRA
 UVF
  UTV
   BBC
    RUC
    MI5

                    DUP
                  Sinn Fein
                Mortar -launcher
                Mother of
                    Disappeared kids,
                        Interned brothers.

Here, we are again the then;
Polluted, pollinated by a rotten spew of seedling that
Invaded,
  Infected,
    Infested,
      Degraded,
        Digested,
          Devoured
            Detained
A generation who must aspire to shake-off the shackles,
Break the very spinal column and
Decapitate
The rotten rent-a-mob of what occurs on a daily basis;
With fucking flag and fag and gob,
On dole and benefits and healthcare and cash-in-

hand

And water rate and free winter gas and take away chippy vacuum,

Down-the-casino Monday morning.

The eternal lullaby of poverty, of idleness.

To envisage, foresee, dream beyond the red brick emptiness,

To light aflame the swollen larvae

and suffocate itself in a cocoon of its own flesh and gut.

Yet, we see pressed shirt on TV and polka-dotted-tied assembly fool,

Dictating policy and bill to a room

Where deep down, they know the dirty truth, we know it too:

poverty pays well–

Filthy gold.

Sinner Know Thy Name
by Uhene

Oh, sinner, what's your name?
What corruption is your game?
Don't play me that way.
For while our rebellion is the same,
Destruction is *your* shame,

Die, Die, Die. Die to self,
Live, Live, Live for God.
Put on Christ the Lord,
For Sinner, it is your name.
Sinning has become your fame, and
Judgement your claim.

Die, Die, Die!
We need to confess

We're the one's to blame.
Because of living,
Life lame.
How confused you are to be the same.
So Die, Die, Die . Die to self
Live for God.

Put on Christ the Lord.

Just don't live in vain .

Believe that the Almighty Creator

Has the Power to save and provide refuge .

Do yourself the favor and REPENT!!!

A Ship Without Anchor
by Teuta S. Rizaj

A ship without anchor gets tired by endless sails—
Riding on the waves: now joy, then sadness.

Oh, the sweetest Peace, Shalom, Salam,
If the surface knows no calm
I'd better be a drowned clown!

It can be so dry in here:
The land's open; exposed to wind.
Spring's barren; no water to drink!

Yet you can be a veracious friend
When no one can be trusted.

You can be a kind companion
When roads are empty and forlorn.

You can be a constant confidant
When the walls have ears.

You can be a brother, a sister
When the rains keep falling.

Yes, you can be an angel, a true human being
When the winds keep blowing, destroying.

Autumn's Embers
by Thomas Koron

The season that once burned has now grown cold,
And nature has left stains upon the leaves.
I see colors of red, orange and gold,
As they roll off of my shoulders and sleeves.
They collect in small piles on the ground
In picture perfect images of fall.
Wind causes them to scatter all around,
While I rake them together wide and tall.
I watch birds assembling on a wire,
Before they all fly south until next year.
Shivering while I sit close to a fire,
I find myself now loathing winter's near.
    While snow falls during the cold Decembers,
    I keep warm recalling autumn's embers.

Unforgiving Winter
by Thomas Koron

The wind whispers curses into the trees,
As I look out the windows of my room.
Snow keeps falling through the relentless breeze,
And the sky's a prison of darkened gloom.
Thin ice has now covered much of the earth,
With our lakes getting frozen all around.
Harsh winds work at delaying spring's rebirth,
Causing the trees to sway above the ground.
Sensing the cold air surging up my spine,
My body shutters from the chilling blast.
I see animals scurry up a pine,
As another day flees into the past.
    I've found myself trapped right in the center
    Of this cruel and unforgiving winter.

Upon Enquiring of a Teacher
by C. P. Little

I got asked a question that stuck with me;
Where does poetry happen?

The obvious answer is on the page,
The logical answer is in the conscience,
The sentimental answer is in the heart
The egotistical answer is in the soul,
The emotional answer is in the gut,
The metaphysical answer is in the cosmos,
The conscientious answer is in society,
The obnoxious answer is in the hook and reel,
The passionate answer is in love and death,
The timeless answer is in the palm of your hand,
The flippant answer is in the vacuum of emptiness,
The academic answer is in the fabric of language,
The contemporary answer is in empty adjectives,
The mathematic answer is in rhythm and meter,
The revolutionary answer is in stirring rebellion,
The creationist answer is in God's interminable
light,
The inspirational answer is everywhere, always.

I got asked a question that stuck with me;
Where does poetry happen?

The truthful answer is actually very simple indeed.

Helen R. Davis

Helen Davis is the award-winning author of the novel CLEOPATRA UNCONQUERED (Savant 2015) about an alternate world in which Cleopatra and Antony are victorious at Actium.

High School High
by Helen R. Davis

2001 to 2005
The years of High School High
Supposed to be the best years of your life?
If that is the case, someone lied!

Began all right
And I had some fun times
But the teachers and staff believed
That High School was the rest of your life
I was told I would be nothing
For I was not prom or homecoming queen

Little did they know within me were greater queens
Who needs the prom queen
When you can be Queen of Egypt
And bring the men of Rome to your knees?
Four years in which I dreamed of a life outside the
Prison walls of the high school.
Every day I waited for the bell to ring so I could go
home
 I may not have been prom queen
But I would be Queen of Egypt

And I would visit lands far away
Far away from their drama

We won the state championship in football
And I celebrated with my friends
For I was happy for them
Yet the next year while my friends
Chatted about Bennifer
I got to visit Montreal
And made the French world home
To my Egypt

Pain and loss the last two years
I lost my Madame and two classmates
Who while I did not know them well
I felt the pain of my friends who
Were saddened and shocked by their loss
Graduation time rolled around and I could not wait
Anxious to leave, I was told I would not make it
For I was told I had no place in the world
All the best wishes were given the queen of the
prom

Yet I did. I pulled through and left the school be-
hind

Proms, homecoming dances
A world long gone
The friends I miss but not the times

Graduation parties told it all
The lies of the institution
My party with ten friends,
We danced, sang, and were so happy it was over
We were so glad our term was over

Yet the prom queen's party was a wake
For being queen of the prom is fleeting
I care little for tiny tiaras
For I prefer the crook and flail of Egypt
And the crowns of Europe
And the adoring cries of the Argentine people
Sorry, High School High
You were wrong

Through the halls of my high school
Next year will be the 10 year reunion
And I will not attend
For I plan to be in Montreal again

France and The Holy Land await in the wings

Keep your dances to yourself

For I will rule nations

And you will rule only the football field

The Science of School
by Dylan DiMarchi

We go everyday
Doing the same things
On the same schedule

But succeeding is a skill
A challenge
A part of the game of youth

A few letters of the alphabet
Decide the fates of our lives
A soup of destiny
Seasoned with the spice of life

It's like a tempting buffet
Too much of one, too little of another
Overwhelms the senses
But the perfect balance satisfies

We try to fill our plates
With an appetizer of friends
A main course of smarts
And a dessert of sports

Nourishing the body, mind, and soul

Temptations abound
Choose wisely
The seeds we sow now
Will feed us in the future

On Poetry
by Dylan DiMarchi

You think you're so smart
So sly
So cunning
Tricking my hungry mind
With your odd phrases
And twisted mazes

I seek that inner meaning
Driving me to keep reading
But there is deception
Hiding empty words
Only ink on a page

You're a sham
An imposter
Author of smoke and mirrors
Leading a hunt for gold and riches
Inside a treasure chest
Overflowing with vast nothingness

Doc Krinberg

Doc Krinberg is a California native who has in his life been a sailor, a strip club barker, taxi driver and doctor of education. Previous works have been published by Savant in FIFTY-EIGHT STONES and BELLWETHER MESSAGES

After a Fine Night
by Doc Krinberg

Sunrise, a flashlight
thick smoke in a primeval bog
Morning in L.A.

Red lightning eyes blink
storm behind them has ebbed
All the whiskeys gone

Leg out of the sheet
post-mortem on breathalyzer sex
Her cadaver turns and smiles

I'm
by Teuta S. Rizaj

I'm given food in a golden plate, but I'm
hungry
I'm handed water in the silver cup, but I'm
thirsty.

I'm given shelter, but I'm homeless
I'm beseeched by knowledge, but I know
nothing.

I'm given parents, but I'm orphan
I'm blessed with friends, but I'm alone.

But if I have You, I'll be Whole
But if I have You, I'll be You.

Kaethe Kauffman

Kaethe Kauffman has her Ph.D. in Art History and is an Associate Professor of Art. She has taught at the University of California, Irvine and at Chaminade University in Honolulu among other universities. She has innovated inter-disciplinary team-taught courses: Art and Writing and Art and Psychology. She has a book of humorous short stories awaiting publication in early 2016.

Dad in a Photo
by Kaethe Kauffman

Not cast by him, a shadow follows Dad.

It belongs to another entity that trails him,
this Marine, this man of Secret Service.

Straight lines march behind his head, one
after another: do this, do that, do it now, do
it tomorrow, go to war, marry the fuming
pixie, arrest those men, scream away the
wounds, get this house, then that one, make
three babies in six years, grow a huge gar-
den to feed everyone, guard Roosevelt,
Truman and Eisenhower.

By age forty, it is too much; time speeds
away from him.

No wonder he loves to fish, to stand for
hours in a stream, dreaming with the under-
water creatures.

He looks to the distance with his mouth
open, waiting.

What does he see with eyes shaded by an overhanging brow, thick with dense black hair?

Behind his head is a window divided into twelve panes, openings to the next world.

He falls through the third glassy panel when the shadow breaks his body too soon.

Now his heart exists free of shade.

Family
by J. Okajima

Family…
You don't have to be blood related
To be a true family in today's world.
There are so many people whom are
What others consider to be good friends
But in reality they are nothing but family.
It never matters if every time you call is for
money,
Just as long as you call.
Everyone in your family does these things
for love
So don't ever feel bad about asking
For we know that it will be paid back in one
form or another!!
We aren't friends, we are Family!!

Yo soy a ti, Estados Unidos
by Helen R. Davis

Argentina, the land of Eva Peron
For a time the land of *mis sueños*
Argentina, España, *las tierras desconocidas*
Para una chica de Ohio

I was looking for Eva Peron,
The woman who inspired me
I also loved Isabella, *madre de los Americas*
The best thing Spain has produced
Strong woman, *fuerte, madre de España y mujer de Fernando*
Antes de Cleopatra, era Isabella!

En España Isabella was the queen who haunted me
I loved her boldness and strength
A working mother and queen in a time in which women
Were ornaments is not hard to like.
I did not have time to visit her *tumba* in Granada.
Lo siento, mi querida Isabel!

In Spain I found Eva's park and lived near

Her husband's old residence and
Found *un chico español* who sold me
A book about Eva's husband.

I told him "I will write a novel about Evita" *en castellano*
la lengua de mis sueños
He told me "*Cuando tú lo escribes, lo venderé!*
Argentina, la patria de Evita
Una tierra maravillosa para mi
At least for the primera vez"
Time *ha pasado* and I returned home

I was looking for Evita but found myself.
As dear as Argentina is to me, I returned with an amor
For my own *patria—Estados Unidos*
Travel is a gift and lovely
But I no longer am ashamed of my home

Egypt replaced Argentina as I began to write of
La Victoria de Cleopatra
Argentina y España son
memorias distintas de una otra chica

I now dream of Cleopatra's day,
and of Paris and Jerusalem
As opposed to Evita the Lady of Hope
And Isabella of Spain

Other queens have replaced Isabel, past and mod-
ern.
My Anglo Saxon roots remain and are strongly in
place
But Argentina and Spain came first
And as always, the US is my home and freedom.
I love this nation all the more for my travels.
Dios bendiga a Espana y Argentina
And, of course, God bless the US and UK.

                    - to the girl who never will be again

Noffke's Tunnel
by C. P. Little

Sometime before dawn,
Persian-rose horizon hovering,
Threatening daybreak,

Winter exhales satisfied -
Wisping the brutal sleet along
Iceglass-paved *Mühlenstraße*;
pinching our flesh goose-bumped.

This hinterland mauer.
This death-strip.
Who is "Pankow?"
Young Noffke, left East.
Sebastianstraße tunnel.

Noffke's only wish is just beyond,
A death-wish within our eye-line;
Safe in the "way back when"
Safe in the comfort of "back then,"
Safe in Kreuzberg.

I have drifted West to East,

Late in the Berlin night,
Through the cruel gentle snow
With Noffke's tunnel under
My boots, beneath my soles.

And all his dreams;
His *Hannelore*,
His Rainer.

Last Night I Caught Myself
by Teuta S. Rizaj

Last night I caught myself thinking of you—
beautiful thoughts, adorned with rubies and sap-
phires: Our first meeting, the job interview, you and
Mark;
a tiny windowless office, expanding, seeing into
the infinite ocean of Oneness.

The warm waves of thoughts, past merging into
present.
I smile—the prayer rug under my weight lifts up its
head
and smiles back.

The living room, the amber glass door slides in
front of
me into the room of living memories. Time lowers
its
wing, yielding to timeless Love—and then,
Love alone exists.

Lines Composed Upon a Visit to My Brother's Grave
by C. P. Little

I have flowed through night opaque,
To observe the rust and gold glimmer,
Disperse and renew into the darkness.

Ours is the black country.

The night here as a noise; a voice,
That grows and swells from below;
Eddie and ebb into the darkness.

Ours is the black country.

Black, svelte trunks of tired elm,
Leaveless, silhouetted dusk-on-black,
Lining out the back into the darkness.

Ours in the black country.

Shapeless and moist, the air does
Remind us that up there kinetics and
Full emptiness roar into the darkness.

Ours is the black country.

Magpie by two tiptoeing skip-hop across
My brother's grave, two for joy, to lift
Grief-soaked spirit up into the darkness.

Ours is the black country.

A towering vacuum roars deafening below
The tree-top, the conifer and bluebell,
Scalding them in flame into the darkness.

Ours is the black country.

Fandango darkened clouds rest upon
Roslea horizon; midnight-sun dreamless,
To hush-sigh a last breath into the darkness.

Ours is the black country.

Sorry
by J. Okajima

I am sorry

For breaking your heart!

I am sorry

For making you cry

Over the accusations I made against you.

I am sorry

For playing with your heart

Because I felt that I couldn't love you any

more,

But actually I was scared to get hurt again.

I am sorry

For causing so much misery

With all the lies spun.

My own head was spinning

And nothing seemed real any more,

Not even the beating of my own heart.

Please forgive me

In my own stupidity

I walked away from something that could've

been

Such a good, tight knit family.

Daniel S. Janik

Daniel S. Janik's multi-award-winning collected poems appear in three volumes, FOOTPRINTS, SMILES AND LITTLE WHITE LIES (Savant 2008), THE ILLUSTRATED MIDDLE EARTH (Savant 2008) and LAST AND FINAL HARVEST (Savant 2008), and in various regional, national and international poetry anthologies and collections. A 2007 Poet of the Year, he is also author of the innovative children's books, A WHALE'S TALE (Savant 2008) and THE TURTLE DANCES (Savant 2013), and is known worldwide for his pioneering educational work, UNLOCK THE GENIUS WITHIN (Rowman & Littlefied, 2005), and for his two-Telly-award-winning documentary, CLEAN WATER, COMMON GROUND (National Film Network, 1999) on the state of the world's water.

http://janik.yolasite.com

Walls
by Daniel S. Janik

What beautiful walls these
That shelter me in the night,
Yet,
If a shelf from the outside cold,
Then also a shelter from all that's warm
Except a God or Goddess's heart
Who knows no bounds
Except the walls of the heart.

It is a sacrilege to pray within the these
walls.
If only I could kneel
Upon a floor of dirt and mud,
I could bow my heart
And cry the soul-tears
(I've forgotten how to cry human tears)
And know my searching
At last
is over.

If I had my way…
If I had

I would tear down the protective walls

If I had my way...
I would tear down this house,
This building,
This town,
This city,
This society that protects me
From the God or Goddess

If I had my way...
I would destroy our spectacles of science,
Possess what can't be seen,

If I had my way...
I would, once again, crawl like the beasts

If I had my way...
I wouldn't give a God-damn about this cal-
lous world

I would tear this building down
If I had my way...

But I don't.

When What is True is Also Real
by Danny Smith

Paths crossed like stars at night
Carried on in streaks of light
Moving past yesterday
Who knew it would be this way
I see you and you do me
I miss the old day's simplicity
No excuses it is what it is
A delay in fortunes and certain bliss
But time shall come I know this to be
I feel it with the utmost certainty
That what is meant shall come to me
A treasure unlike any I have yet to see
And then two hearts will again feel
When what is true is also real
And colors oh the colors will shine
Some not seen for a long, long time
And blessings and joy shall finally come
Not in a dream but from where they're from
And contentment will find me and fill my
heart
Oh this so prayed for to finally start...

I Love You
by J. Okajima

I Love You is more than just words to say to
your lover
It represents how your heart beats
Each time you see your lover
It holds you together through those tough
times
When your love is away on deployment
Or when they have passed on into the heav-
ens all to soon!

Do you see love in the air
Or has Love vanished
As being replaced by technology
Instead of spoken meaningful words?

I see people without much love
Held in their eyes and hearts any more,
Being too busy working or checking their
mail.
They flirt and scan the crowd for something
better

Yet the best thing is the person in front of
them
Holding out their hands for a longing em-
brace.

Open your eyes to see this love
Before it is too late
And they have flown away to the heavens...

Dead Awake
by Doc Krinberg

Room unfocused
Murky, a photo in stopbath
Undeveloped

Next to me
Blurry, in the sheet shadow reliefs
Breathing

Streetlight's glow
Shaded, drapes in muted disarray
Struggling

Nightstand busy
Cluttered, apothecary's nightmare
Excuses

Escrow
by Daniel S. Janik

I have learned, said he,
I have learned over these many years
Things your heart doesn't know to cry over
yet.

I have learned, said he,
All life is born in common water.
Seaworthy ships prepared only for storms
fail in the doldrums.

I have learned
That diatom or whale,
Both feed in the same ravenous sea.

I have learned, he began,
Then shook his head at my disbelief,
Laid it on my shoulder
Cried
And died.

He Rides Above the Clouds
by Thomas Koron

He rides above the clouds with no shadow,
Through the peaceful land of eternal sleep,
With all of his fellow bikers in tow.

Always keeping an eye on those below,
May all who have known him no longer weep—
He rides above the clouds with no shadow.

Moving swiftly, forever on the go—
Rising above hills, no matter how steep,
With all of his fellow bikers in tow.

He treasures your friendship more than you know;
May his company you forever keep—
He rides above the clouds with no shadow.

The sun reflects brightly off his window—
Through Lexington, the motorcycles sweep,
With all of his fellow bikers in tow.

He watches you all riding in a row,
Holding your memories of him so deep.

He rides above the clouds with no shadow,
With all of his fellow bikers in tow.

To the memory of Chad DeLoy.

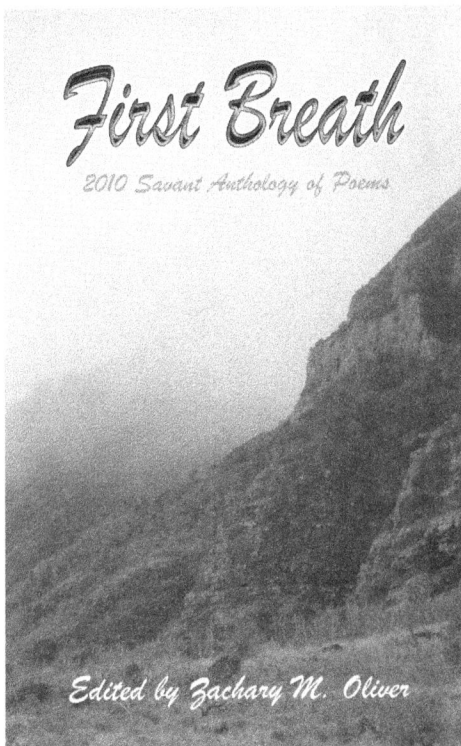

**First Breath - 2010 Savant Anthology of Poems
(2010)**
Zachary M. Oliver (Editor)
72 pp. 8.25" x 5" Softcover
ISBN 978-0-9845552-2-2
*Twenty-nine poems by ten outstanding poets and writers
selected for their outstanding merit, including Helen
Doan, Erin L. George, Jack Howard, Daniel S. Janik,
Scott Mastro, Zachary M. Oliver, Francis H. Powell,
Gabjirel Ra, V. Bright Saigal and Orest Stocco.*

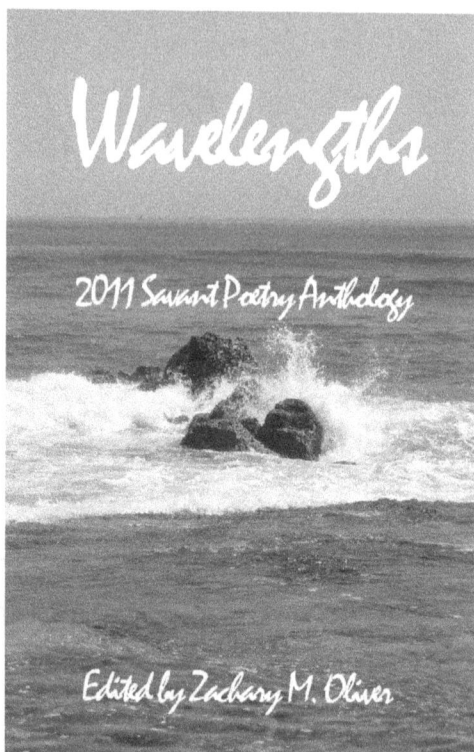

Wavelengths - 2011 Savant Poetry Anthology (2011)
Zachary M. Oliver (Editor)
102 pp; 5.25" x 8" Softcover
ISBN 978-0-9829987-6-2

Thirty-eight poems by sixteen outstanding poets and writers including Four Arrows, Penny Lynn Cates, J. R. Coleman, Nadia Cox, Helen Doan, Erin L George, IKO, Daniel S. Janik, Vivekanand Jha, A. K. Kelly, Zachary M. Oliver, Cara Richardson, Michael Shorb, Jason Sturner, Jean Yamasaki Toyama and Jeremy Ussher.
LONDON BOOK FESTIVAL AWARD

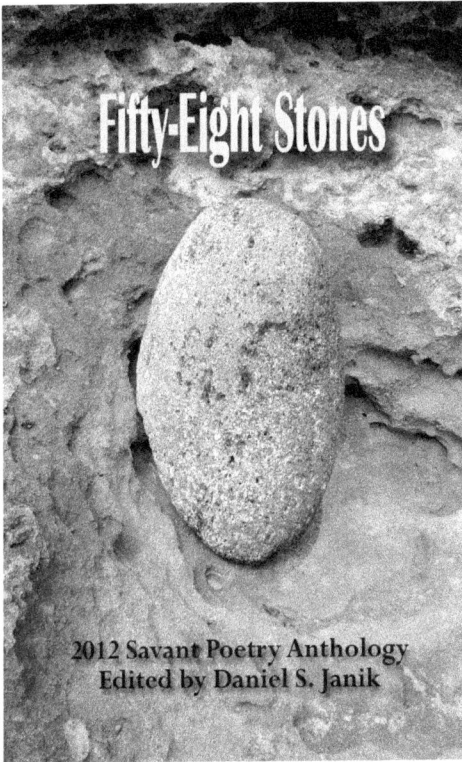

Fifty-Eight Stones - 2012 Savant Poetry Anthology
(2012)
Daniel S. Janik (Editor)
128 pp. - 5.25" x 8" Softcover
ISBN 978-0-9852506-5-2

Thirty-four outstanding poems by eleven exceptional and many award-winning poets including Shawn Canon, Nadia Cox, Helen Doan, David Gemmell, Richard Hookway, Daniel S. Janik, Vivekanand Jha, Doc Krinberg, Julie McKinney, Francis Powell and Jean Yamasaki Toyama.

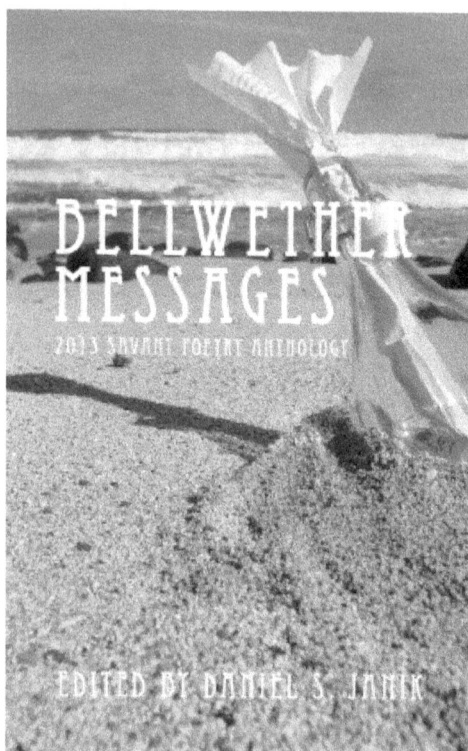

Bellwether Messages - 2013 Savant Poetry Anthology (2013)

Daniel S. Janik (Editor)

134 pp. 5.25" x 8" Softcover Pocketbook

ISBN 978-0-9886640-4-3

Thirty-two selected poems by fourteen outstanding poets including Tender Bastard, Shawn P. Canon, Natascha Hoover, IKO, Daniel S. Janik, Vivekanand Jha, Thomas Koron, Doc Krinberg, Cathal Patrick Little, Peter Mallett, Emma Myles, Ken Rasti, Uhene' and Ashley Vaughan.

LONDON BOOK FESTIVAL AWARD

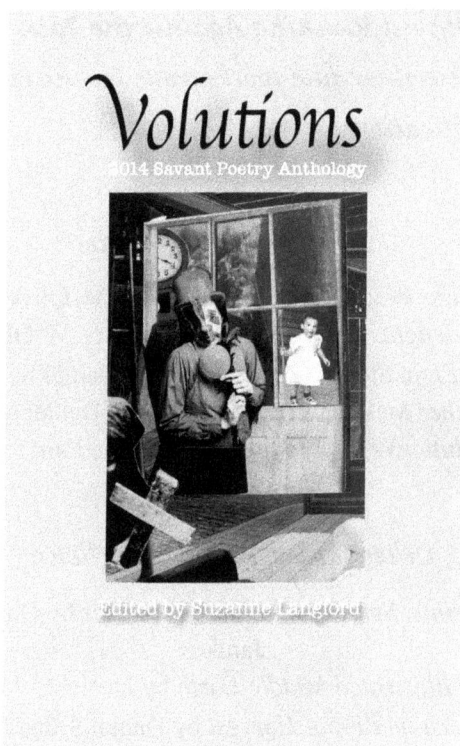

Volutions - 2014 Savant Poetry Anthology (2014)

Suzanne Langford (Editor)

146 pp. 5.25" x 8" Softcover Pocketbook

ISBN 978-0-9915622-1-3

Thirty-six exceptional poems by fourteen outstanding poets including Noemi Villagrana Barragan, Elsha Bohnert, Hans Brinckmann, Helen R. Davis, K. Lauren de Boer, Duandino, Lonner F. Holden, Daniel S. Janik, Kaethe Kauffman, Suzanne Langford, Lucretia Leong, C. P. Little, Leilani Madison and Lady Mariposa.

LA, LONDON, PARIS and PACFIC RIM BOOK FESTIVAL AWARDS

If you enjoyed **Running Against the Pack**, consider these other fine works from Savant Books and Publications:

Savant Poetry Anthologies:

First Breath (2010) edited by Z. M. Oliver
Wavelengths (2011) edited by Zachary M. Oliver
Fifty-Eight Stones (2012) edited by Daniel S. Janik
Bellwether Messages (2013) edited by Daniel S. Janik
Volutions (2014) edited by Suzanne Langford

Other Savant Poetry Collections:

Footprints, Smiles and Little White Lies by Daniel S. Janik
The Illustrated Middle Earth by Daniel S. Janik
Last and Final Harvest by Daniel S. Janik

Other Savant Books and Publications:

Essay, Essay, Essay by Yasuo Kobachi
Aloha from Coffee Island by Walter Miyanari
A Whale's Tale by Daniel S. Janik
Tropic of California by R. Page Kaufman
Tropic of California (the companion music CD) by R. Page Kaufman
The Village Curtain by Tony Tame
Dare to Love in Oz by William Maltese
The Interzone by Tatsuyuki Kobayashi
Today I Am a Man by Larry Rodness
The Bahrain Conspiracy by Bentley Gates
Called Home by Gloria Schumann
Kanaka Blues by Mike Farris
Poor Rich by Jean Blasiar
Ammon's Horn by Guerrino Amati
The Jumper Chronicles by W. C. Peever
William Maltese's Flicker by William Maltese
My Unborn Child by Orest Stocco
Last Song of the Whales by Four Arrows
Perilous Panacea by Ronald Klueh
Falling but Fulfilled by Zachary M. Oliver
Mythical Voyage by Robin Ymer
Hello, Norma Jean by Sue Dolleris
Richer by Jean Blasiar
Manifest Intent by Mike Farris
Charlie No Face by David B. Seaburn
Number One Bestseller by Brian Morley
My Two Wives and Three Husbands by S. Stanley Gordon
In Dire Straits by Jim Currie
Wretched Land by Mila Komarnisky
Chan Kim by Ilan Herman
Who's Killing All the Lawyers? by A. G. Hayes
Ammon's Horn by G. Amati
Almost Paradise by Laurie Hanan
Communion by Jean Blasiar and Jonathan Marcantoni
The Oil Man by Leon Puissegur
Random Views of Asia from the Mid-Pacific by William E. Sharp
The Isla Vista Crucible by Reilly Ridgell
Blood Money by Scott Mastro
In the Himalayan Nights by Anoop Chandola
On My Behalf by Helen Doan
Traveler's Rest by Jonathan Marcantoni
Keys in the River by Tendai Mwanaka
Chimney Bluffs by David B. Seaburn

www.ingramcontent.com/pod-product-compliance
Lightning Source LLC
Chambersburg PA
CBHW060130050426
42448CB00010B/2045

* 9 7 8 0 9 9 6 3 2 5 5 5 4 *